LITECOIN

The Ultimate Guide To The World Of Litecoin

Ikuya Takashima

Copyright © 2018 Ikuya Takashima

All rights reserved.

ISBN: 1986181235
ISBN-13: 9781986181235

CONTENTS

Chapter One: Introduction To Litecoin 1

Chapter Two: How Litecoin Works 17

Chapter Three: How To Buy Litecoins 28

Chapter Four: Litecoin Wallets – Keeping Your Litecoins Safe 49

Chapter Five: Everything You Need To Know About Litecoin Mining 60

Chapter Six: Understanding The Impact Of SegWit And Lightning Network On Litecoin 78

Chapter Seven: The Future Of Litecoin 89

Chapter Eight: Should You Invest In Litecoin? 103

Conclusion 115

Other Ikuya Takashima books availabe on Amazon. .. 117

About The Author 118

Introduction

For the everyday person who does not dream of code and programming every night, the world of cryptocurrencies might seem complex, confusing, and intimidating. However, it doesn't have to be that way. With the right information, you will quickly understand how cryptocurrencies work and how you can invest in them and potentially make yourself some money. With the most popular cryptocurrencies like Bitcoin exploding in value, getting into the game is becoming increasingly expensive. If you want to make money, you should consider alternatives to Bitcoin. One of these is Litecoin, which was among the first cryptocurrencies to be created after Bitcoin. This book will teach you everything you need to know about Litecoin. You will learn what Litecoin is, why it was created, some of its basic features, how you can get ahold of Litecoins, how to keep your Litecoins secure, and whether it is a good investment or not.

Let's get started!.

Chapter One: Introduction To Litecoin

The last year saw a great surge in the popularity and public awareness of cryptocurrencies. Most of this hype was driven by the massive rocketing in the price of Bitcoin, the world's first cryptocurrency. While Bitcoin remains the most well-known cryptocurrency, there are several other popular and promising cryptocurrencies. One of this is Litecoin. Litecoin is an advanced, next-generation digital currency that allows anonymous and heavily encrypted transactions between people across a peer-to-peer (P2P) network. Like most other cryptocurrencies, Litecoin is based on blockchain technology and is not backed or controlled by any government, central bank, or central authority. Litecoin is an open source cryptocurrency, which means that anyone has the right to study its code, modify it, and distribute the software as they wish and for any purposes. Like any other currency, Litecoin can be offered in exchange for goods and services.

Litecoin was released on 7 October 2011, two years after the release of Bitcoin. It was created by a former Google programmer known as Charles Lee in a bid to fix some of the shortcomings and challenges he saw in Bitcoin. Litecoin was created, or 'forked', from Bitcoin's source code, which means there are some similarities between Litecoin and Bitcoin. Since Litecoin is an offshoot of Bitcoin, it would be impossible to completely understand Litecoin without comparing the two. Therefore, there will several references to Bitcoin in this book. According to its creator, Litecoin was created to be the silver to Bitcoin's gold. Where Bitcoin is seen as the 'digital gold', as a store of value, Litecoin aims to be the 'digital silver' than can be used for daily transactions.

Despite having started from very humble origins and only having a few subtle technical improvements over its big brother, Litecoin has also experienced massive growth to become the sixth largest cryptocurrency by market cap. To put the growth of Litecoin in context, I will compare it to the growth of Bitcoin. In 2017, the price of Bitcoin rose by over 1,800%, from below $1,000 in January to a few hundred dollars shy of $20,000 by the close of the year. While this might seem astronomical, it is nothing compared to the price of Litecoin, which rose by over 9,000% in the same period, starting at about $4 in January and hitting $371 by the end of the year. Litecoin currently has a market cap of about $10 billion.

Why Was Litecoin Created?

Soon after Bitcoin was launched, it faced some challenges affecting its adoption. One of these problems was that Bitcoin had long transaction times. In addition, the mining of Bitcoin was not considered fair. It was skewed to favor large mining pools who had access to advanced mining ASICs (Application Specific Integrated Circuits). This meant that everyday people could not mine the cryptocurrency using their desktop computers. Luckily, Bitcoin's software was open source, which meant that anybody could alter its original codebase, add whatever features they felt were necessary, and create a new cryptocurrency. Lee realized that there was need to create a cryptocurrency that solved the problems of Bitcoin, so made some minor changes to Bitcoin's code and Litecoin was born.

One of the first things that Lee did to was to improve the transaction speed. Technically, cryptocurrency transactions are instantaneous. However, time is required for the other computers in the cryptocurrency's blockchain network to confirm the transaction. At its inception, transaction on the Bitcoin network took roughly 10 minutes. Lee improved the transaction speed of Litecoin to about 2.5 minutes, or four times faster than Bitcoin. The greatest advantage of a faster speed is that it allows the network to handle higher transaction volumes as more users join the network. By making Litecoin faster, Lee also wanted to make Litecoin more attractive to merchants. This is because a merchant taking Litecoin payments can confirm four transactions in the same time it takes a merchant using Bitcoin to confirm one transaction. The faster transaction time also means that the Litecoin network is less susceptible to double spending attacks as compared to Bitcoin.

The second and most fundamental change that Lee made in was to change the Proof-of-Work algorithm used by

Litecoin. For both the Bitcoin and Litecoin networks, new coins are created through the process of mining. In this process, some computers in the network allocate their processing power to verify and confirm the transactions made by other users. They do this by solving difficult mathematical puzzles which are governed by cryptographic algorithms. In exchange for this service, they earn newly created units of the cryptocurrency. (The process of mining will be discussed in greater detail in Chapter Five.)

Bitcoin employs a Proof-of-Work mining system that relies on the SHA256 algorithm. In the early stages of Bitcoin, people could use CPUs and GPUs to mine Bitcoin. However, the calculations of the SHA256 algorithm can be significantly accelerated using parallel processing. As mining competition increased, ASICs with vast parallel processing capabilities were developed to mine Bitcoin. This made it next to impossible to mine for Bitcoin using CPUs and GPUs. Unfortunately, ASICs are insanely expensive and use vast amounts of power. Therefore, those who could afford to buy and operate the ASICs quickly became Bitcoin mining monopolies.

Lee did not want the same to happen to Litecoin, so he decided to implement Scrypt as the Proof-of-Work algorithm for Litecoin instead of SHA256. The aim was to make processor intensive mining more difficult and expensive for Litecoin. Scrypt has more serialized calculations and requires large amounts of Random Access Memory, something that ASIC miners do not have in plenty. This makes mining for Litecoin using ASICs inefficient, which in turn means that miners with ASICs cannot monopolize the network. To effectively mine for Litecoins, miners use CPUs and GPUs. By implementing the Scrypt algorithm, Lee made Litecoin more accessible to everyone, thus making the network more decentralized.

The other major difference between Bitcoin and Litecoin is the number of coins that can be generated. When Bitcoin was created, its inventor capped the maximum number of coins that could be released into the network at 21 million coins. Lee, on the other hand, set 84 million coins as the maximum number of Litecoins that will ever be generated. Despite having a maximum number of coins that will ever be in circulation, both Litecoin and Bitcoin are divisible into very small units, which means that they can still be used to pay for low-priced goods and services, regardless of the overall price of a single unit. However, since Litecoin has a higher number of coins that will ever be generated, and since it currently has a lower price than Bitcoin, it is more suited for daily use, while Bitcoin is more suited to be used as a store of value due to its high price. This is in alignment with Litecoin's vision of becoming the 'digital silver'.

A Brief History Of Litecoin

Soon after Bitcoin was launched, Charles Lee, who was working at Google at the time, heard about it and immediately understood that this was something that held significant promise. According to Lee, cryptocurrency was going to transform the financial sector in the same way that the internet revolutionized access to information. Greatly enthused with this new idea, Lee started mining Bitcoin. Around this time, people started launching new cryptocurrencies. Lee did not want to be left behind, so he created a cryptocurrency known as Fairbrix in September 2011.

Fairbrix was created as a clone of another cryptocurrency known as Tenebrix. Tenebrix had also been launched in 2011. However, the launch of Tenebrix had been greatly mismanaged. In a bid to enrich himself, the developer of Tenebrix pre-mined seven million coins for himself before releasing the software to the public. However, people were wary of supporting Tenebrix, and many called for the development of a Tenebrix clone that would have zero pre-mined coins to make it fair. Lee took up the challenge of creating a fair Tenebrix clone, and that is how Fairbrix was born.

Developing Fairbrix was Lee's first attempt at using the Scrypt Proof-of-Work algorithm, which would make it more difficult for miners using ASICs to dominate the network. However, Fairbrix did not become successful. This was because of a bug in the client used by Fairbrix that prevented several of the initial Fairbrix blocks from generating more coins. Fairbrix was also hit by a 51% attack. 51% attacks occur when one person gains or controls more than 51% of the total mining capacity of a cryptocurrency. 51% attacks are easy to launch in the early days of a new cryptocurrency because the network does not usually have enough miners.

After the failure of Fairbrix, Lee went on to create Litecoin, which became an instant success. To prevent being plagued by the same bug that contributed to Fairbrix's failure, he used some code from Bitcoin's client, with some major differences to make Litecoin more technically advanced. He also used the Scrypt algorithm to make mining more accessible to the everyday person. In order to prevent the 51% attack that killed Fairbrix, Lee announced Litecoin's genesis block about a week after releasing the Litecoin source code to the public. During that week, people could mine Litecoin on Testnet, a kind of sandbox where people can test cryptocurrencies without earning any reward and without adding the transactions to a live blockchain. By so doing, Lee generated some hype for Litecoin and showed its advantages before the genesis block was announced. By the time the genesis block was announced a week later, the network had enough miners to keep it protected from a 51% attack.

In November 2013, the Litecoin development team released version 0.8.5.1, which fixed some of the previous version's vulnerabilities and enhanced security. Following the release of version 0.8.5.1, the price of Litecoin saw a 100% growth in 24 hours, allowing Litecoin to reach a market cap of $1 billion. In December 2013, version 0.8.6.1 was released, improving Litecoin's performance and security and lowering the transaction fees. In April 2014, the development team released version 0.8.7.1, which provided more fixes to existing security bugs. In 2017, Litecoin implemented an upgrade known as SegWit (Segregated Witness), which solved some challenges concerning transaction fees, scalability, and interoperability. 2017 also saw the first cross-chain atomic swap between Litecoin and Bitcoin, which means that users can now instantly exchange Litecoins for bitcoins without going through a third party.

The Team Behind Litecoin

The success of a cryptocurrency depends a lot on the team behind the cryptocurrency. While the essence of a digital currency is to provide decentralization, without a leader, it might be challenging for the community to make meaningful progress. For instance, despite deciding to disappear from the face of the earth, Bitcoin's founder Satoshi Nakamoto provided leadership and guidance during the early days of the cryptocurrency until it gained traction. By the time he/she left, Bitcoin was too big to fail. Luckily, Litecoin has a very strong leadership in the form of its founder, Charles Lee. Vocal and knowledgeable, Lee has been very critical to the growth of Litecoin. He has helped push the implementation of various technological upgrades on the network. With someone like Lee explaining the importance of making such upgrades and how they should be implemented, the Litecoin community is more cooperative and united towards the achievement of Litecoin's vision.

Apart from Charles Lee, Litecoin has another lead developer known as Warren Togami and a team of voluntary developers from its huge community. In 2016, Litecoin managed to acquire a full-time developer known as Shaolinfry. Unfortunately, Shaolinfry left Litecoin in 2017. However, being a community-driven project, there's no shortage of developers to help with the implementation of upgrades. In addition, being a spin-off of Bitcoin, many of the upgrades developed for Bitcoin can be adapted to

Litecoin as well. Lee and the Litecoin community have a healthy relationship with the Bitcoin development team, communicating every now and then to share ideas. With such a dedicated leader and community, you can bet that Litecoin will continue seeing the growth it has seen since its inception.

Litecoin Features

Litecoin is characterized by the following features:

Open Source Software

Just like its bigger brother, the Litecoin software is open source. Litecoin was also released in a transparent process that allowed users and other interested parties to independently verify its binaries and their corresponding source code. Litecoin was released under the MIT/X11 license, which allows users to freely use, copy, modify, and distribute the source code. Users can also distribute modified versions of the source code.

Blockchain

Like Bitcoin and most other cryptocurrencies, Litecoin is based on blockchain technology. The blockchain is a like a public ledger that holds a record of all the transactions that have ever taken place on the Litecoin network. The records are permanent; once a record has been made, it can never be altered. The records can be viewed by anyone within the Litecoin network. One unique feature about the Litecoin blockchain is that it supports a higher transaction volume than the Bitcoin blockchain. This is because the Litecoin blockchain generates blocks about four times faster than the Bitcoin blockchain. Recently, Litecoin implemented SegWit and Lightning upgrades. While Lightning is still undergoing trials, once complete, it will allow the Litecoin network to confirm transactions up to eight times faster than Bitcoin. This makes Litecoin more attractive to merchants because of the faster confirmation times and lower transaction fees.

Anonymity

Litecoin maintains the same kind of anonymity you would expect from cryptocurrencies. Your Litecoin wallet is not linked to personally identifiable information like your name or physical address. This means that you can make Litecoin transactions while keeping your identity anonymous.

Industry Integration

Since Litecoin was created by modifying Bitcoin's source code, it shares a lot of characteristics with Bitcoin. Therefore, it is supported by many of the applications and services that support Bitcoin. This explains why Litecoin is among the most well-integrated altcoins. Behind Litecoin is a very loyal and passionate community. It is also supported by varying sectors in the cryptocurrency industry, including developers, cryptocurrency exchanges, ATMs, online and offline merchants, and web casinos.

Decentralization

Litecoin is a decentralized digital currency, which means that it is not controlled or regulated by any government, central bank, or central authority. Instead, everything is controlled by all the computers within the network which process and validate transactions. However, Litecoin takes decentralization a notch farther. Unlike cryptocurrencies like Bitcoin, where large mining pools have monopolized mining using expensive and power consuming ASICs, Litecoin is relatively ASIC-resistant, which means that mining is accessible to anyone with a good CPU or a GPU.

Speed

One of the main advantages of Litecoin over Bitcoin is that it generates blocks four times faster than Bitcoin. This allows the Litecoin network to validate transactions faster and support a higher volume of transactions. In May 2017, after the implementation of the SegWit upgrade, Litecoin was able to make a transfer from Zurich to San Francisco using the Lightning Network. The Lightning Network is still undergoing trials. Once it's completed, Litecoin transactions will become instantaneous.

Widely Available Resources

General information about Litecoin is widely available, as is a list of services and exchanges that support the cryptocurrency. The Litecoin Block Explorer Charts provides real-time stats about the Litecoin network, while the Litecoin Wiki contains lots of general information. The Litecoin source code is also available to any interested parties through Github..

Chapter Two: How Litecoin Works

If you are new to the world of cryptocurrencies, everything might seem overly technical, confusing, and complicated. You have probably asked yourself the following questions: how does Litecoin work? If Litecoins are just some pieces of data, why can't I just copy and paste my Litecoins to double them? What keeps the whole system secure? In this chapter, I am going to give you a detailed breakdown of how the Litecoin network works. I will do this by explaining seven concepts that govern how Litecoin works. It's important to note that since Litecoin forked off Bitcoin, it has lots in common with the Bitcoin network.

Decentralization

Like most other cryptocurrencies, Litecoin is decentralized. This means that no one in the Litecoin network holds the power to make decisions or play an oversight role. Instead, this power is delegated and distributed to all the computers that form the network. Since there is no central authority, there has to be a set of rules that govern how the different computers in the network interact with each other. Broken down to its simplest form, the Litecoin network is simply a protocol that is guided by mathematical rules. All the computers in the network have to follow these rules. These rules determine every aspect of the network, including the transactions. For a transaction to be considered valid, all the computers in the network have to agree that the transaction took place. If they cannot agree, then the transaction is rejected. This ensures the integrity of the network even in the absence of a central oversight entity.

Distributed Systems

The Litecoin network is a distributed system, which means that it is not located in any one central location or server.

Instead, the same version of the network is distributed across multiple individual computers that are interconnected with each other. Despite being separate and autonomous, all these computers work toward a common goal. Since the network is a distributed system, it has no single point of failure. Hackers cannot bring down the network by attacking a single computer. Similarly, the network remains unaffected even if some computers in the network go offline, since the others will continue running the network.

Cryptographic Encryption

Encryption is the process through which data or information is converted into secret code in order to prevent unauthorized persons from accessing the content of the data. When you send Litecoins, you do not send any actual coins. Instead, what you send are bits of data or information. To prevent other people from accessing your Litecoins or altering your transactions, there's need for a system to ensure that the Litecoins (data) that you send through the internet are only accessible to authorized persons (the sender and the recipient). The Litecoin network, as well as most other cryptocurrency networks, ensures the security of this data through cryptographic encryption. It uses the rules of mathematics and cryptography to convert the data into secret code (encrypted files) that can only be accessed by someone who has the correct key that is necessary to decrypt the data. By so doing, the network is able to keep the transactions secure.

Most common forms of encryption use a single key to encrypt and decrypt data. This means that both the sender and the recipient can access this data. However, most cryptocurrencies, including Litecoin, use two separate keys, one to encrypt the data and another to decrypt the data. When a transaction is made on the Litecoin network, two keys are generated – a private and a public key. The public key is used to encrypt the data. To decrypt it, you need the private key. This explains why Litecoin transactions are irreversible. After the sender has encrypted the transaction data, they no longer have access to it because they don't have the private key. Compare it to a door that requires two separate keys to lock and unlock it. If the two keys are held by separate people, if one locks the door, even accidentally, there is no way they can unlock it without the permission of the other.

In the Litecoin network, the public key is what we know as the Litecoin wallet address. By sending Litecoins to the wallet address, the sender basically encrypts data (Litecoins) and sends it to the recipient. Only the person with the right private key (the wallet owner) can access and use the Litecoins. The sender has no way of retrieving them since they don't have the private key.

Transaction

The transfer of Litecoins from one wallet to another is what is known as a transaction. When you send Litecoins to another person, your Litecoin wallet generates a string of data that is encrypted using the recipient's public key or wallet address. The data string is broadcasted to the Litecoin network pending confirmation that the transaction has actually taken place. Confirmation is provided by the recipient's wallet through some form of mathematical proof. The proof is also broadcasted to the network. The data string and mathematical proof are checked by the computers in the network. If the majority of the computers confirm that the transaction has indeed occurred, the transaction is added to the immutable public ledger known as the blockchain.

A Litecoin transaction is made up of three components. The first one is the input. The input consists of the transaction ID and a list of outputs from past transactions. The transaction ID is a hash of the previous transaction block. The list of outputs from past transactions is necessary since the Litecoins from those transactions are going to be sent in the current transaction. The second component is the output, which is a list of the numbers of Litecoins being sent and the recipient addresses. The last component is the signature required to spend the Litecoins. By sending Litecoins to another person, your wallet generates a Signature showing that you have signed off your Litecoins to the recipient.

The Blockchain

The blockchain is the foundation on which Litecoin – as well as most other cryptocurrencies – is built. In its simplest form, the blockchain is basically a database that is distributed across a network and that is publicly accessible. The database contains a list of all Litecoin transactions that have ever taken place since Litecoin was released to the public. These transactions are grouped together into blocks, which are essentially all the transactions that took place within a given time frame. In the case of Litecoin, blocks contain a list of transactions that take place every 2.5 minutes. The blocks are added to the database in chronological order, with each block being added on top of the previous one, forming a chain of blocks. Each Litecoin block is made up of a hash that refers to the previous block, the transaction data of all the transactions in the block, and a time stamp.

Since the Litecoin network is a distributed system, no single computer holds a master copy of the blockchain. All the computers in the network simultaneously hold the latest version of the blockchain. This makes the Litecoin network transparent, since everyone has the same copy of the blockchain. In addition, any changes are confirmed by all the computers in the network and automatically updated to each of them. The greatest advantage of this is that it becomes next to impossible to corrupt the Litecoin blockchain. If you make changes in one computer, the other computers will reject the change. Therefore, to corrupt the blockchain, an attacker would need to take control of more than half of the computers in the Litecoin network. This is what is known as a 51% attack. However, the possibility of this happening practically is next to impossible.

Nodes

The individual computers that make up the Litecoin network are referred to as 'nodes'. For a computer to become a node, it needs to download and run the Litecoin blockchain protocol. This allows the computer to connect with other nodes within the network. Nodes are a very important part in the Litecoin network. They play the role of network administrators. It is their responsibility to confirm the validity of all the transactions that take place within the network as well as to record the transactions onto the public database. Nodes are also tasked with adding complete blocks onto the Litecoin blockchain. Anytime a new computer joins the Litecoin network, it receives the latest version of the blockchain. This allows it to start communicating with other computers on the network and to perform the tasks of a node.

Like we noted earlier, whenever a person sends Litecoins to another, a data string is generated and broadcast to the network. Nodes look at this data string and confirm that all elements of the transaction are valid by comparing the transaction data with data from previous transactions. The aim is to make sure that the Litecoins have not been double spent. In the event that a node finds the data string to be invalid, it automatically rejects the transaction. The node that sent the transaction is marked as a non-trustworthy node. All the other nodes in the network orphan it and ban it from the network, helping to keep the network secure.

However, if the data string from the transaction is confirmed to be valid, the node forwards the transaction to miners. The role of miners is to group transactions into blocks. I will discuss this in greater detail in the next section. Once miners group the transactions into blocks, they pass them back to the nodes for validation. Again, the nodes compare the block data to previous blocks, and if everything checks out, the block gets added to the blockchain.

Mining

The process of validating Litecoin transactions, grouping them into blocks, and adding them to the Litecoin blockchain is what is referred to as mining. This is also the process that creates and releases new Litecoins into the network. Basically, mining involves providing bookkeeping services to the network to ensure that all the transactions are valid. In return for the services, miners are rewarded with the transaction fees charged to users, as well as newly generated Litecoins. Anyone can become a Litecoin miner. For those who want to get into mining, I will discuss the requirements and process of mining Litecoin in Chapter Five.

To verify Litecoin transactions, miners have to solve complex and computationally intensive mathematical puzzles. However, unlike Bitcoin mining, these puzzles are not based on the SHA256 algorithm. Instead, Litecoin's mathematical puzzles are based on a different hashing algorithm known as Scrypt. Unlike the SHA256 algorithm, which relies on raw processing capacity, the Scrypt algorithm relies more on Random Access Memory, which makes it possible even for people without specialized equipment to mine Litecoin. The first miner to solve these equations is given the responsibility of adding the next block to the chain. In return, the miner earns the transaction fees charged for the transactions and any newly generated Litecoins.

Litecoin has an upper limit of 84 million coins. This means that once 84 million Litecoins have been mined, there will be no new Litecoins produced. To control the rate of production of new Litecoins, Litecoin uses the same approach as Bitcoin. Just like Bitcoin, the Litecoin block reward gets reduced by half every time a certain number of blocks are mined. In the same way Lee increased the maximum production of Litecoins from 21 million to 84 million, he also quadrupled the number of blocks needed for halving of the block reward. Therefore, the Litecoin block reward gets cut in half after every 840,000 blocks. This takes an average of about 4 years. The first halving of the Litecoin block reward occurred in August 2015, reducing the block reward to 25 Litecoins. The next one is expected to take place in August 2019. This will reduce the Litecoin block reward to 12.5 Litecoins per block.

Chapter Three: How To Buy Litecoins

Now that you have a clear understanding of what Litecoin is, we can go ahead and look at how you can buy your first Litecoins. In this chapter, I will show you the payment methods that you can use to pay for Litecoins, some reliable places where you can buy your Litecoins, and how to choose the best Litecoin exchange.

Available Methods For Paying For Litecoins

Bank transfer: One of the easiest ways of paying for Litecoins is using good old bank transfer. Several cryptocurrency exchanges allow buyers to pay for Litecoins through bank transfers. You simply need to wire the funds to the exchange and specify the amount of Litecoins you want to buy. Once the payment is processed, the exchange will send the specified number of Litecoins to your Litecoin wallet. It's good to note that bank transfers are a slow method of paying for Litecoins, since it might take a couple of days for the transaction to be processed. This is critical, since Litecoins are very volatile. As you wait a couple of days for the transaction to go through, the price of Litecoin might have appreciated or depreciated by over 100%.

Credit card: While this is a common online payment method, it is not widely accepted by Litecoin exchanges, due to the fact that Litecoin transactions are irreversible. Credit card payments are susceptible to charge backs, which would lead to the exchange losing money. However, you can still use credit card payments to purchase Litecoins from exchanges such as Coinbase, Coinmama, Indacoin, and 247exchange. It is good to note that most exchanges tend to charge a higher price for credit card payments.

PayPal: Just like with credit cards, most Litecoin exchanges do not accept PayPal payments due to the risk of chargebacks. However, you can still use PayPal payments to pay for Litecoins on exchanges like Cryptex24. Alternatively, you can use PayPal to purchase bitcoins from the VirWox exchange and then use the bitcoins to pay for Litecoins on an exchange of your choice.

Bitcoin: One of the most common methods of paying for Litecoins is exchanging them for Bitcoin or other altcoins. To do this, you first need to purchase bitcoins and then convert them into Litecoins. You can purchase bitcoins from exchanges, P2P networks, or Bitcoin ATMs.

Other payment methods: There are several other methods that you can use to pay for your Litecoins. Some exchanges support other online payment methods like Skrill, Sofort, iDEal, etc. You can also pay for Litecoins using cash. Coinmama allows you to make a cash transfer via Western Union in exchange for Litecoins. If you are using a peer-to-peer network like Litecoinloca.net, you can arrange to meet the seller and pay them directly in cash. Exchanges like 247exchange also allow you to exchange cash for a prepaid voucher that you can use to pay for Litecoins.

Where To Buy Litecoins

Once you have decided on how you are going to pay for your Litecoins, the next step is to find a suitable place to purchase them. The most common places where you can purchase Litecoins are:

Exchange platforms: These are online platforms Like Coinbase, Coinmama, BitPanda, and so on. They each act as an escrow service, holding Litecoins, fiat money, and other cryptocurrencies. If you intend to frequently buy large amounts of Litecoins, you should consider buying through an exchange platform. Exchange platforms usually have fair prices, as well as fairly low transaction fees and spreads. The major disadvantage of purchasing Litecoins through an exchange platform is that you will required to provide personally identifiable information, making them a poor option if you want to purchase your Litecoins anonymously.

Brokers and direct commercial exchanges: These are online platforms that perform the same role as traditional currency exchanges. However, instead of dealing strictly with fiat money, they allow you to exchange fiat money or other cryptocurrencies like Bitcoin for Litecoin. Brokers and direct commercial exchanges offer one of the simplest ways of purchasing Litecoins.

Peer-to-peer networks: These are online platforms that bring together Litecoin buyers and sellers, without performing the role of a middleman. P2P networks charge relatively low transaction fees. Litecoins prices are also fairly low, usually determined by market forces and liquidity. The most popular Litecoin P2P network is Litecoinlocal.net, which brings together Litecoin buyers and sellers from the same town or city. The two can then transact on their own terms, using their preferred mode of payment.

How To Select The Best Litecoin Exchanges

There are numerous cryptocurrency exchanges that support Litecoin. With so many to choose from, it can be a bit challenging for a beginner to choose the best one to use. Below is a list of factors that you should keep in mind when selecting a Litecoin exchange:

Basic exchange information: The first thing to consider is some basic information about the exchange, such as its founder, where it is located, and the section of the market it caters to. Avoid using exchanges that have anonymous owners who cannot be researched. The location of the exchange matters because different countries have different laws and regulations regarding cryptocurrencies. While many countries are yet to develop any formal laws around cryptocurrencies, the passing of such laws will have an impact on an exchange based within the country.

Supported currencies and liquidity: Avoid going for exchanges that support only one type of cryptocurrency. For instance, avoid an exchange that only supports Litecoin. Instead, opt for exchanges that support multiple trading pairs. A good example is Coinbase, which supports multiple pairs such as LTC/USD, LTC/BTC and LTC/ETH. This means that you can get Litecoins in exchange to fiat money (USD), as well as other cryptocurrencies like Bitcoin and Ethereum. You should also consider the exchange's liquidity. The higher the liquidity (high trading volume), the better the exchange.

User-friendliness: If possible, you should opt for exchanges that are easy-to-use even for beginners, with simple, intuitive interfaces, quick loading times, and compatibility with both desktop and mobile devices.

Trading fees: Exchanges make money by charging users for every transaction that is carried out on the platform. The transaction fee is usually a small percentage of the total transaction amount. To save some money and get the most value, you should use exchanges that have the lowest trading fees. Some exchanges even have a flexible fee structure where the fee decreases as your monthly trading volume increases.

Customer support: The world of cryptocurrencies is constantly evolving, with new technologies getting added each day. In such a dynamic environment, many beginners sometimes find the processes complex and confusing. To avoid making mistakes that cost you time and money, go for an exchange that has helpful and experienced customer support who are always ready to help out users.

Security: Remember, your Litecoins are equivalent to the amount of money you spent to buy them, so you should be careful about their security. You don't want to lose your money as a result of an exchange getting hacked. To avoid this, check to ensure that an exchange is committed to ensuring the safety of your money before you buy from them.

User experience: The best way to ascertain the quality of an exchange is to find out what other users are saying about the exchange. Join Litecoin blogs and forums and find out what others are saying about each exchange. Which one do they recommend? You wouldn't want to use an exchange when other people are complaining about the quality of its service.

If you keep the above factors in mind when choosing a Litecoin exchange, you will no doubt end up with one that best suits your needs.

Best Exchanges To Buy Litecoin

Keeping these factors in mind, here are some of the best exchanges where you can buy Litecoins:

Coinbase

This is one of the world's most popular cryptocurrency exchanges, with users running into the millions. The US-based exchange was started in 2012 and supports most popular cryptocurrencies like Bitcoin, Ethereum, and Litecoin. The popularity of Coinbase stems from its good reputation, user-friendliness, and good security. Its fees are also quite reasonable. Coinbase allows you to pay for Litecoins using Visa and MasterCard credit and debit cards.

It's important to note that Coinbase only works with cards that support '3D Secure', a new standard in online payments security. You can find out if you card supports '3D Secure' by adding it to Coinbase. If you get an error message, then it doesn't. Currently, Coinbase is available in only 32 countries. If the service is available in your country, you can instantly purchase Litecoins from Coinbase through the following steps:

- Go to the Coinbase website and register for a new account.
- Provide a photo of your government-issued ID for verification purposes.
- Navigate to the payment methods page and select the 'Add Payment Method' button.
- Choose your card type and add the details of your card. Coinbase will then make two small transactions on your card.

- Go to your card's account and note the amounts in the above transactions. Enter these amounts into the provided entry field in the Coinbase website to verify your card. You should now be ready to purchase your first Litecoins.
- Go to your account dashboard and select Litecoin.
- Click on the Buy/Sell tab and key in the amount of Litecoins you want to purchase.
- Select 'Card' as the payment method and confirm that everything is okay. Click on the 'Complete Buy' button to complete the transaction. You will receive the Litecoins on your Coinbase account in a few minutes. It's important to note that Coinbase charges a 3.99% standard fee on all purchases made through credit/debit cards.

You can also purchase Litecoins from Coinbase through a bank transfer. Coinbase provides two ways of doing this: Direct Buy and Depositing to USD Wallet. When you sign up for a Coinbase account, you are given the option of creating a USD Wallet. You can transfer money from your bank into your Coinbase USD Wallet and then use this money to pay for Litecoins. However, it's good to note that transferring money into your Coinbase USD Wallet takes several days — about 4 or 5. When dealing with cryptocurrencies, this is a very long time. A lot can happen in 4 days. Cryptocurrencies are very volatile, and prices can shoot or drop 100% in just one day. Therefore, you should not use this method when you want a quick buy. However, once the money has been transferred to your USD Wallet, you can make instant buys.

The other option is to make a direct buy. Similar to depositing money into your USD Wallet, it will take 4-5 days for the Litecoins you paid for to reflect in your wallet. This is because it takes the same amount of time for the bank to process the transaction and send the money to Coinbase. However, with a direct buy, you do not have to worry about price volatility. When you make a direct buy, the Litecoins are locked at the current price. You get the Litecoins at the price you bought them at even if the price rises or drops before they reflect on your wallet. This is a good option when you think that the price of Litecoins will go up in the next few days, and when you are totally confident that the price will not drop in the short term. In such a situation, if the price of Litecoin rises, you will make some profit even before the Litecoins reflect on your wallet. Similarly, if the price goes down, you will suffer some loss even before the Litecoins reflect on your account.

Finally, you can also buy Litecoins through the GDAX (Global Digital Assets Exchange). This is a cryptocurrency trading platform that is owned by Coinbase. Here, you buy the Litecoins from other traders, instead of buying from Coinbase itself. Both of you have to agree on the price for a trade to take place. You can use your Coinbase credentials to log into the GDAX. Buying your Litecoins on GDAX has an advantage over buying directly from Coinbase. Once you have deposited money into your GDAX account, you can choose to buy Litecoins at market price or limit price.

When you choose to buy Litecoins at market price, the GDAX will make the trade based on the minimum sell order placed by another trader. For instance, if the minimum sell order placed by a trader is $237, you will get Litecoins at that price. In this case, you are referred to as the Taker, because the other trader made an offer and you took it. On the other hand, if you choose to buy at limit price, you will be required to set a limit price. Let's assume that you have set you limit price as $235. In this case, the trade will only take place when another trader agrees to sell their Litecoins at your limit price, i.e. $235. In this case, you are referred to as the Maker, since you made an offer and the other trader took it. When buying Litecoins through GDAX, you are charged 0% fees if you are the Maker, while the fees vary between 0.10% and 0.30% if you are the Taker.

BitFinex

BitFinex is a Hong Kong-based cryptocurrency exchange that has been in operation since 2014. BitFinex allows users to buy and sell several cryptocurrencies, including Bitcoin, Litecoin, Ethereum, Monero, Zcash, Ripple, and many other popular altcoins. You can pay for Litecoins on BitFinex using either USD or bitcoins. To purchase Litecoins using USD, you will have to pay a wire fee of at least $20, as well as a transaction fee of between 0.1% and 0.8%. BitFinex also charges a small fee whenever you deposit or withdraw money/cryptocurrencies from your BitFinex account.

To get started with BitFinex, you will need to register for a new account and provide photos of your government-issued ID for verification purposes. Identity verification usually takes 15-20 days after you submit your verification documents. BitFinex is available on browsers as well as on an Android and iOS mobile app. After some changes to the service, BitFinex is no longer available to customers within the United States.

Binance

Binance is a fairly new cryptocurrency exchange that has been seeing very rapid growth. Binance currently supports over 100 different types of cryptocurrencies, including Litecoin. The process of registering on Binance is fast, simple, and straightforward. However, you will still be required to provide a valid ID for verification purposes. One of the most attractive things about buying your Litecoins from Binance is that they have very low transaction fees. They charge a 0.1% standard trading fee on all trades, which is way less than what most other cryptocurrencies charge for transactions. If you want to reduce your fees even further, you can do so by using

Binance Coin (BNB), which is a new cryptocurrency that is native to Binance. Trades who use BNB are eligible to discounts of up to 50%. Binance is available on mobile for both Android and iOS devices and has multilingual support, with more than five languages supported.

Kraken

Kraken is another big and popular cryptocurrency exchange that has been in operation since 2011. The San Francisco based exchange aspires to be the world's first cryptocurrency bank. Kraken's popularity stems from its good reputation, intuitive and feature-rich user interface, low deposit and transaction fees, low spreads, worldwide availability, and great customer support. Kraken supports a wide variety of cryptocurrencies, including Bitcoin, Litecoin, Ethereum, Ethereum Classic, Zcash, Stellar, Monero, Ripple, ICONOMI, Dogecoin, Augur, Gnosis, and so many more. Kraken also supports a wide variety of fiat currencies, including US Dollars, Euros, British Pounds, Canadian Dollars, and Japanese Yen. Kraken allows you to buy Litecoin in exchange for any of the above fiat currencies. You can make the payments via wire transfer or SEPA. Unfortunately, Kraken does not support credit/debit card payments at the moment.

Another good thing with Kraken is that it is security conscious, with support for two-factor authentication, PGP/GPG email signing and encryption, as well as a master key for account recovery in case you lose your passwords. Unfortunately, getting verified on Kraken can take some time, since you have pass through three tiers of verification. However, all this is meant to ensure the security of your funds and to prevent financial malpractices.

Changelly

If you live in a country that is not supported by other exchanges like Coinbase and Kraken, you can easily purchase your Litecoins from Changelly, which is available in almost every country in the world. Changelly allows you to pay for Litecoins through your credit/debit card. Alternatively, you can get Litecoins in exchange for bitcoins or any other altcoins.

Signing up for an account on Changelly is pretty easy and straightforward. However, you need to have a MasterCard/Visa credit or debit card. Changelly supports the native currencies of most countries. However, these will first be converted to their USD equivalents before you can use them to buy Litecoins.

To buy Litecoins on Changelly using a credit card, you should follow the following steps:

- Head over to the Changelly homepage where you will see two fields showing fiat currencies on one side and cryptocurrencies on the other side. Select USD on the left field and select Litecoin on the right field.
- Check and confirm the rate and the number of Litecoins you are going to receive.
- Enter you Litecoin wallet address.
- Once again, confirm that all the payment details are correct and then click on the 'Create Transaction' button. By doing so, you agree with Changelly's terms and conditions.
- After the transaction is created, click on the 'Pay with Visa/MasterCard' button. Changelly processes

card transaction through London-based Indacoin Limited.

- Enter your card details. For your card to work, it needs to support '3D Secure'. After entering the card details, enter a phone number that is attached to your credit/debit card.
- You will receive a phone call, which will give you a digital code. You will enter this code on the order page.
- Head over to your online banking app and find a bank statement with a 3-digit Indacoin code. In case you cannot find the statement, click the 'Record' button and record a voice clip of yourself saying "Indacoin verification." Send this along with a photo of you and your ID or passport.
- After entering the code or sending the voice recording together with your picture and passport, wait a few minutes until the transaction is processed. You will receive your Litecoins and receipt in about 5-30 minutes.

To buy Litecoins on Changelly using Bitcoin, follow the following steps:

- Head over to the Changelly homepage, where you will see two fields showing different cryptocurrencies on either side. Select Bitcoin on the left field and select Litecoin on the right field.

- Enter the amount of bitcoins you want to exchange and click the 'Exchange' button. This will take you to a page showing the exchange rate and the amount of Litecoins you are going to get.

- Once you have confirmed that everything is correct and satisfactory, click on 'Next'.

- You will be taken to a page asking you to enter the address for the wallet where you intend to receive your Litecoins. Enter your wallet address and click on 'Next'.

- You will be shown all the details of the transaction again. Confirm that everything is correct. Once you are sure that everything is correct, select the 'Confirm and Make Payment' button.

- You will be taken to a page showing the wallet address where you need to send the bitcoins. This will be in the form of the actual address as well as

QR code. You need to make the deposit as one transaction.

After sending your bitcoins to the provided address, the transaction might take anywhere between a few minutes and an hour to be processed. Once processing is done, you will receive the specified number of Litecoins in your Litecoin wallet, as well as an email notification of the transaction.

Poloniex

This is another cryptocurrency exchange that has gained massive popularity among cryptocurrency enthusiasts and traders. Poloniex has been around for a while, having been founded in January 2014 by Tristan D'Agosta. The US-based exchange supports Bitcoin, Litecoin, and hundreds of other altcoins. Getting started with Poloniex is easy and quick. Most people love Poloniex because it has a user-friendly and intuitive user interface while at the same time offering a feature rich platform that has complex analysis tools for more advanced traders. Poloniex also has great support, coupled with very low trading fees. However, Poloniex offers no support for fiat currencies, which means that you cannot exchange your dollars for Litecoin. Instead, you will need to convert your dollars into Bitcoin and then use the bitcoins to pay for Litecoin.

As I mentioned before, there are many other exchanges out there where you can buy Litecoins, with many more coming up every now and then. However, the exchanges discussed above are some of the best options available.

Chapter Four: Litecoin Wallets – Keeping Your Litecoins Safe

I have mentioned Litecoin wallets several times, and if you are new to cryptocurrencies, you might be wondering what a Litecoin wallet actually is. Being a digital cryptocurrency, Litecoin cannot be stored the same way you normally store your fiat currency notes. Instead, Litecoins can only be stored in a digital wallet, which is essentially a software program or computer application that keeps track of the amount of Litecoins you own. It also allows you access your Litecoins and conduct various transactions, such as receiving or sending Litecoins. You can think of a Litecoin wallet as some kind of email program. However, instead of sending and receiving email messages, a wallet allows you to send and receive money in the form of Litecoins. In the same way an email program allows you to access all your previous email messages, a wallet also allows you to access a history of all your Litecoin transactions. You cannot make any Litecoin transactions – including sending or receiving Litecoins – without a wallet. Your Litecoin wallet will be a very important tool for keeping your Litecoins safe, therefore you should take some time to ensure you are well-versed with wallets.

Types Of Litecoin Wallets

There are different types of Litecoin wallets, each with its own advantages and disadvantages.

Online wallets: These are wallets that keep your Litecoins on someone else's server. They are also referred to as cloud wallets. People use online wallets because of their unrivaled convenience. Since they store your Litecoins on an online server, you can access your Litecoins from anywhere in the world, provided you have an internet connection. Sending Litecoins from an online wallet is easy and very convenient. However, since they store your Litecoins on the cloud, online wallets are the least secure. They are the most susceptible to hacking attacks. You should secure your online wallet with a very strong password. You should also avoid accessing your online wallet on publicly-shared computers and devices.

Desktop and mobile wallets: These are wallets that store your Litecoins on your desktop computer or mobile device. Most of them are very user friendly. They are also more secure than cloud wallets. Mobile wallets are more convenient than desktop wallets, since you almost always have your mobile device with you. To make transactions from a desktop wallet, you need access to your desktop computer, which you do not have the luxury of carrying around with you. Apart from using a strong password on your mobile/desktop wallet, you should also write down your seed phrase and keep it safe. This will help you recover your Litecoins in case you lose access to your desktop computer or mobile device.

Offline wallets: Also referred to as cold wallets, these are wallets that do not store your Litecoins on a computer or other devices that has an internet connection. Since they cannot be accessed over the internet, cold wallets tend to be more secure than hot wallets (those that are stored on a device with an internet connection, such as online and mobile/desktop wallets).

There are two types of cold wallets: paper wallets and hardware wallets. Paper wallets are wallets that store the security key to your Litecoins on a piece of paper. For someone to steal your Litecoins, they need to get their hands on that piece of paper. However, paper wallets are very inconvenient, since you cannot make any transactions from your paper wallet. Instead, you need to upload your Litecoins to a hot wallet before making any transactions. You need to be careful while uploading them to a hot wallet to avoid negating the security advantages of the paper wallet. You should also keep in mind that losing the piece of paper means losing your Litecoins.

Hardware wallets, on the other hand, store your Litecoins on a device that looks like a USB flash drive. Since your Litecoins are not accessible over the internet, hardware wallets are very secure. They are also password protected for extra security. This means that even if someone steals your hardware key, they cannot access your Litecoins without the correct password. You should keep the seed of your hardware wallet safely to help you recover your

Litecoins in the event that you lose your hardware wallet. You should also note that unlike the other kinds of wallets, hardware wallets are not free. You have to buy them.

Best Litecoin Wallets

Here are some of the best wallets for you to safely store your Litecoins:

Coinbase

Apart from being an online exchange where you can buy and sell your Litecoins, Coinbase also provides you with a wallet where you can keep your Litecoins. The Coinbase wallet is available both as an online wallet as well as a mobile wallet, with apps supported by both Android and iOS devices. Despite being a hot wallet, Coinbase offers a fairly decent level of security. Your Litecoins are stored in offline mode, which minimizes the risk of getting stolen by hackers. Coinbase also uses two-factor authentication before you can access your Litecoins. Coinbase also gives you a high level of control, with support for multi-signature wallets. In additions, the Coinbase wallet gives you access to the Coinbase exchange, which means that apart from storing your Litecoins, you can also buy or sell them from the wallet.

Ledger Nano S

This is a very popular and one of the most trusted hardware wallet that you can use to safely store you Litecoins. Since it is a cold wallet, you do not have to worry about some malicious hacker getting access to your private keys and stealing your Litecoins. The Ledger Nano S comes with an inbuilt OLED screen that allows you to carry out some transactions independently, without having to connect it to a computer. This eliminates the risk of someone gaining access to your keys while the device is connected to the computer. The device also has a pin code feature, which provides a second layer of security. Apart from Litecoin, the Ledger Nano S supports many other cryptocurrencies, including Bitcoin, Ethereum and Ethereum Classic, Ripple, Dash, Dogecoin, Zcash, Komodo, Stratis, and many more. The Ledger Nano S costs about $65.

Trezor

When you talk about hardware wallets, this is among the best that come to mind. The product of a Czech-based company known as SatoshiLabs, the Trezor has malware-resistant software, which keeps it safe even in the event that you connect it to an infected computer. The Trezor works well with Windows, OSX, and Linux, and is one of the best options for storing your Litecoins. Apart from Litecoin, Trezor also supports several other popular cryptocurrencies, such as Bitcoin, Namecoin, Dash, Ethereum and Ethereum Classic, Doge, and Zcash. Just like the Ledger Nano S, the Trezor has a small OLED screen that allows you to perform some operations in an offline environment. The Trezor goes for about $99.

Exodus

This is one of my favorite desktop wallets. Exodus is a versatile, intuitive, and beginner-friendly wallet that supports several other cryptocurrencies in addition to Litecoin. Exodus does not store your private keys online. Instead, the keys (and therefore, your Litecoins) are stored on your computer's hard drive. One of the best things about Exodus is that despite being user friendly even to beginners, it does not compromise on security. It also has a one click recovery system that allows you to recover access to your wallet and Litecoins in case you lose your password or lose access to your computer. Another thing I love about Exodus is that it comes with the ShapeShift exchange built into it, allowing you to exchange your Litecoins for other cryptocurrencies within the wallet. The Exodus desktop application is available on Windows, Mac, and Linux.

Jaxx

This is another popular wallet that is available both on mobile and desktop devices. Jaxx is a multicurrency wallet, with support for over 10 cryptocurrencies, including Litecoin. Like Exodus, it comes with a 12-word seed phrase back-up feature that allows you to restore your wallet in case you lose access. The interface on the wallet is quite user friendly. Like Exodus, it has also incorporated the ShapeShift exchange into the wallet. The Jaxx mobile app is available for both Android and iOS devices. The desktop app works with Mac and Linux, while Windows users can access it through Chrome and Firefox extensions.

Loaf Wallet

This is a Litecoin mobile wallet that is only available for iOS devices for free through the iOS App Store. The wallet was developed by Charles Lee, the same man who developed Litecoin. This is the first mobile Litecoin wallet that is only available for iOS. The wallet is maintained by a group of volunteers known as the Litecoin Association. Like many other wallets, it uses a 12-word seed phrase which allows users to recover their Litecoins in the event they lose their mobile device or password. Loaf Wallet has a nice innovative feature that allows people to buy Litecoins from Coinbase and transfer them to the wallet.

Litecoin Core

This is the official Litecoin wallet, which is available for free through Litecoin's website. Litecoin Core is a desktop wallet, which means that your private keys and your Litecoins are stored on your computer's hard drive. However, it is good to note that as the official Litecoin wallet, Litecoin Core syncs with the entire Litecoin blockchain. As such, it might take quite some time to sync up everything. It might also take up significant amounts of your computer memory. Litecoin Core is available for Mac, Windows, and Linux.

Electrum-LTC

If you feel that the Litecoin Core wallet is taking a huge toll on your computer, you can switch to Electrum-LTC, which is a lightweight Litecoin desktop wallet that does not have to sync with the entire Litecoin blockchain. This means that synchronization on Electrum-LTC is much faster. The wallet does not take up large chunks of your computer memory either. This wallet is quite up-to-date, and is even SegWit-enabled. It also comes with an extra feature that allows you to freeze an address, which restricts the wallet from sending Litecoins from the specified address. A 12-word seed phrase is used for account recovery. Electrum-LTC is available for Windows, Mac, and Linux.

Liteaddress

If you want the security of a cold wallet but do not want to spend money to buy a hardware wallet, you can head over to liteaddress.org and create a paper wallet for your Litecoins. This generates a Litecoin address for you together with its set of private and public keys, which you can then print on paper and use as a cold wallet for your Litecoins. This is a cheap and almost equally secure alternative to a hardware wallet. It's good to make yourself familiar with the process of setting up a paper wallet as well as precautions you need to take while setting it up. Once you set up your paper wallet, you should also ensure that you keep it safe and secure

Chapter Five: Everything You Need To Know About Litecoin Mining

What Is Mining?

To increase the amount of fiat currency in circulation, the Central Bank simply needs to print more currency. Unlike fiat currencies, Litecoins cannot be printed as need arises. Instead, new Litecoins are generated through a process known as mining. Whenever someone makes a Litecoin transaction, the transaction has to be verified and added to the blockchain. Verification is done by checking the transaction against previous transactions. To do this, computers known as miners have to find solutions to hashes, which are essentially encrypted chunks of data. Finding the solution to the hash proves that the Litecoins in the transaction have not been double-spent. Once the hash has been decrypted or solved, newly generated Litecoins are awarded to whichever miner found the solution to the hash.

Like the Bitcoin blockchain from which it was developed, Litecoin mining uses the proof of work system. This system is energy and time intensive. Despite the huge costs associated with mining, the prospect of winning newly generated Litecoins acts as an incentive for miners to solve these hashes. However, unlike Bitcoin mining, Litecoin does not use the SHA256 hashing algorithm. Instead, it uses the Scrypt algorithm, which makes Litecoin mining significantly different from Bitcoin mining. The Scrypt algorithm allows faster and easier block calculation. Charles Lee utilized the Scrypt algorithm in order to make Litecoin resistant to specialized ASICs, which would lead to the monopolization of Litecoin mining. As Litecoin mining became more popular, some miners developed processors that could mine the Scrypt algorithm more efficiently. However, Litecoin can still be mined using GPUs, though the potential rewards are somewhat lower.

There are no guaranteed results with Litecoin mining, or any other cryptocurrency mining, for that matter. Instead, mining is a competition between miners, with each hoping to be the first one to "discover" the next block. Whoever discovers the block first is awarded with 25 Litecoins. This is known as the block reward. Initially, the miner that discovered the next block first was awarded 50 Litecoins. Charles Lee designed the Litecoin protocol such that the block reward would reduce by half after every 840,000 blocks. The first halving of the block reward took place in August 2015, while the next one is predicted to take place around August 2019. The idea is that the block reward will keep reducing until the number of Litecoins in circulation reaches 84 million, after which no more new Litecoins will be generated.

The Litecoin blockchain has a block generation time of 2.5 minutes. This means that every 2.5 minutes, a miner has the chance to discover a new block and get rewarded with 25 Litecoins. Currently, over 60% of the 84 million Litecoins have been mined. Once all the Litecoins have been released, mining and the addition of new blocks to the blockchain will still continue. There's no limit to the number of blocks that can be added to the Litecoin blockchain. Apart from the prospect of winning new Litecoins, mining is an important part of the Litecoin ecosystem, so some people mine Litecoins as a way to spread the idea and push the adoption of Litecoin.

Litecoin Mining Difficulty

To maintain some consistency in the rate at which new Litecoins are released into the network, the Litecoin blockchain has a system that determines the difficulty of solving the hashes in order for new blocks to be added to the chain. This difficulty adjusts upwards or downwards over time, depending on the amount of effort miners expend into mining Litecoin. The difficulty adjusts by changing the description of the type of target hash that must be produced by the next block. Each hash includes a certain amount of zero characters. The number of zero characters in the target hash is directly proportional to the difficulty. Therefore, the more zero characters in the next target hash, the more difficult it becomes to mine the next block. By adjusting the difficulty, the Litecoin network is able to maintain a block calculation time of 2.5 minutes.

The difficulty of Litecoin mining adjusts itself with every 2,016 blocks that are mined. Mining difficulty is one of the factors that determines the profitability of Litecoin mining. The higher the number of miners, the more difficult it becomes to mine Litecoin. A decrease in the number of miners leads to a decrease in mining difficulty. Going with the current difficulty levels, the last Litecoin will be mined somewhere around the year 2142. As the number of new Litecoins being released into the market decreases, the scarcity will help to prevent inflation in the value of Litecoin.

Imagine a scenario where the price of an ounce of gold shoots from $1,200 to $2,000. Following this increase in price, gold mining companies would increase their production. Some new entrepreneurs might even get into gold mining. This would create extra supply, probably leading to a decline in the price of gold after a while. The situation is different with Litecoin. An increase in price cannot lead to an oversupply of Litecoins. While an increase in price would lead to an increase in mining efforts, the difficulty level would adjust to balance the increased mining efforts, thereby keeping the generation of new Litecoins fairly constant.

There are no restrictions in Litecoin mining. Anyone can join or leave the Litecoin blockchain as they please. If a lot of miners leave the network, the difficulty level will decrease, which will in turn lead to an increase in mining profitability. However, a decrease in the number of effects also has the adverse effect of reducing the overall hashing rate, which will in turn make the blockchain less decentralized. Therefore, the combination of block rewards, cost of mining, and difficulty levels act as a balancing mechanism that maintains the scarcity, value, and integrity of Litecoin.

Litecoin Mining Hardware

If you talk to miners or visit Litecoin mining forums on the internet, you will come across the word 'rigs' often. Rigs are computers that are specifically used for mining. To get into Litecoin mining, you should consider buying one of these rigs. You can still use a personal computer for Litecoin mining. All you need to do is install the right software and join a mining pool. However, it is always better to have a computer that is specifically suited for mining. Your mining computer will keep running for extended periods of time, therefore it needs special setups to keep it cool. Prolonged exposure to high heat will affect the life span of the computer, so it is far better to use a computer that you don't use for other activities and set up some cooing system for it.

One thing you will notice about the Litecoin mining industry is that it is not as advanced as Bitcoin's. While Bitcoin miners have powerful ASICs, most of these cannot be used to mine Litecoin. Remember, Litecoin was built to be ASIC-resistant. However, there are still some specialized Litecoin mining machines.

One machine that is popular among Litecoin miners is the ASIC Scrypt Miner. This is a specialized miner that was developed to increase the efficiency of mining cryptocurrencies powered by the Scrypt hashing algorithm. There are low power ASIC Scrypt Miner models that consume less electricity. Using the low power models can help you maximize your return on investment (ROI).

One of the advantages of using a specialized miner instead of installing mining software on your PC is that the specialized miner is not restricted to mining Litecoin. You can use it to mine other Scrypt-based cryptocurrencies. Some dedicated ASIC Scrypt Miners even allow you to mine two or more cryptocurrencies at the same time. If purchasing a new ASIC Scrypt Miners is too expensive for you, you can opt for a used unit to reduce your starting costs.

Apart from the mining hardware, you will also require some mining software. Luckily, many ASIC Scrypt Miners come with preinstalled mining software. However, if your unit does not come with the software installed, you will need to install the software yourself. Some software options you might consider include:

Cgminer: This is a popular mining program that was originally developed for Bitcoin mining. However, it can still be used for Scrypt-based cryptocurrencies such as Litecoin.

CUDAminer: This is another popular mining software that supports a wide variety of cryptocurrencies, including Litecoin.

CPUminer: This also supports a wide variety of cryptocurrencies, including Litecoin.

If buying specialized mining hardware is not an option for you, then you have two options remaining. You can mine Litecoin using your computer's Central Processing Unit (CPU) or using the Graphics Processing Unit (GPU). The GPU is found on your computer's graphics card. Of the two, mining with the GPU offers better performance and efficiency. If you are totally new to Litecoin mining and do not have a gaming computer equipped with a powerful graphics card, you can still mine Litecoins, though your chances of discovering new blocks will be significantly lower.

To efficiently mine Litecoins using the GPU, you need a dedicated graphics processor, the kind that you might find inside desktop PCs. While many laptops have Intel integrated graphics cards, these are not up to the task for mining. To ensure efficiency and maximum performance, most Litecoin miners build their own dedicated machines with motherboards that support multiple graphics cards. This can be done using riser cables. You should keep in mind that mining is a very system intensive process that will affect the lifespan of your computer's electrical components, so you have to ensure that you have adequate cooling.

Once you have set up your Litecoin mining hardware and installed the necessary mining software, the next step is to set up a wallet to keep all the Litecoins that you win in exchange for providing your hashing power. I covered the topics of Litecoin wallets extensively in the previous chapter, so I won't be going into much detail about wallets in this section.

Mine Alone Or Join A Mining Pool?

Once you decide to get into Litecoin mining, you have the option of going it alone or joining a mining pool. Mining solo seems like an attractive option. You don't have to split the rewards with anyone, which means more Litecoins in your wallet, right? Unfortunately, things are not so straightforward, especially when you are still a beginner in Litecoin mining. Mining alone means you get to enjoy the full rewards, but your chances of success are greatly reduced.

Mining in a pool is more advantageous since the resources of all the miners in the pool are combined, which means that there is a higher likelihood of discovering new blocks. For instance, you may only discover a single block in a year when working alone. The frequency of new block discoveries will increase significantly when you work as a group. Mining in a pool also has a smoother learning curve, since you can offload your frustrations to the pool administrator. Configuring the software for solo mining is also a lot more complicated than with a pool. However, before joining a mining pool, you should take the time to understand how the pool splits and pays the rewards. Here are two common methods employed by most mining pools:

The proportional system: In this system, everyone in the pool contributes their hashing power to the pool. Once a user discovers a new block, the block reward is distributed among all the pool members. The block reward is split among the members in proportion to the number of shares each member has submitted to the pool. However, this method has one major disadvantage. It is quite easy for a member to cheat the system. For instance, some members may engage in 'pool hopping', which is a method that allows miners to maximize their personal profits by exploiting the payment mechanisms of several mining pools.

Per-per-share system: This system does not base its rewards on the number of blocks discovered by the pool. Instead, rewards are based on the number of blocks the group is mathematically expected to find. As such, the members are paid a fixed number of Litecoins. The number is calculated using the mathematical laws of probability. The main advantage of this system is that members are assured of a steady stream of profits without having to wait for the blocks to be actually discovered. However, the risk of this system is borne by the pool operator.

Setting Up Your CPU Miner

This section will teach you how to mine Litecoin using your CPU. Before you can do this, you need to install and configure the mining software. For purposes of this guide, I am going to explain using a Cpuminer, one of the easiest programs to use for CPU mining. The program is available for Windows, Linux, and Mac. In this guide, I will explain using a Windows machine.

The first thing you need to do is to download the program according to your operating system. Once it has downloaded, extract the file to any location on your hard drive, as long as you can remember this location. You will then need to write a simple one-line script (a batch file), which will instruct the mining program on how to run correctly. To create the batch file, you need the following information:

- The path to the location where you extracted the program (path)
- Your mining pool serve 'stratum' URL (stratum URL)
- Your mining server port number (port number)
- The username of your mining pool (pool-username)
- Your worker number or username (worker number)
- Your worker password (worker password)

Using Notepad or any other text editor (avoid using word processors like MS Word), create the batch file using the following formula:

Start *"path"* minerd.exe - - *stratum URL:port number* - a scrypt - - userpass *pool-username.worker number.worker password*

You should replace information in italics with the information that corresponds to your computer and your mining pool. After doing this, save the file with a '.bat' file extension. Navigate to the location where you saved the batch file. Once you double click on it, it will activate your mining program. If your mining pool has a web-based interface, it will come up in a short while, showing that your mining worker is running and active.

Setting Up Your GPU Miner

If you intend to use your GPU or a USB mining device, you won't use the Cpuminer mining software. Instead, you will need to use Cgminer, which is available for free. The program was developed for use by Windows users, though you can still get your hands on unofficial binaries of the program which will work on Mac and Linux. However, it's important to note that Scrypt mining is not supported in the latest versions of Cgminer. Therefore, you should look for an older version that supports Scrypt, which Litecoin runs on.

For purposes of this guide, I am still going to assume you are using a Windows device. However, the process is similar for both Mac and Linux. After downloading the software, extract it to location and note down the address of this location. Before you proceed, ensure that your computer has the latest graphics drivers. Next, open Command Prompt by pressing the 'Win + R', typing 'cmd' and pressing the enter key. Key in 'cd' to change the directory to the location where you extracted the Cgminer software. Type in 'cgminer.exe – n' to bring up a list of all the recognized devices on your PC. Your graphics card should appear in the list of detected devices. As with CPU mining, you will need the following information:

- The path to the location where you extracted the program (path)
- Your mining pool serve 'stratum' URL (stratum URL)
- Your mining server port number (port number)

- The username of your mining pool (pool-username)
- Your worker number or username (worker number)
- Your worker password (worker password)

Again, you will create a batch file using Notepad or another text editor like we did for CPU mining. In this case, you should use the following formula:

Start *"path"* cgminer - - scrypt — *stratum URL:port number* - - userpass *pool-username.worker number.worker password*

Watching Your Miner

Once your preferred mining software is set up and running, several statistics will keep scrolling up the Command Prompt window. Cgminer usually provides more data than Cpuminer. Cgminer will show you information about your mining hardware, the cryptocurrency you are mining (Litecoin, in this case) and the mining pool. Cpuminer will only show your hashing speed as well as data referencing the number of blocks your PC has solved.

Maximizing Your Power

If you have a powerful PC that also has a dedicated graphics card, you can run Cpuminer and cgminer simultaneously. In this case, you should add '- - threads n' to the Cpuminer batch file. The 'n' in this case represents the number of CPU cores that you want to be used in the mining process. You should leave one or two cores free. The free cores will control your GPU. If you use up all cores, no data will be sent to the GPU for processing. Running Cpuminer and cgminer concurrently is a good way to make a comparison between CPU and GPU mining. If you compare the hash rates shown for both mining software, you will realize that the hashing speed of cgminer is almost five times faster than that of Cpuminer.

Litecoin Mining Profitability

There are several Litecoin mining calculators that you can use to see the potential profits you stand to make before you get into mining. The profitability is based on several factors, such as the hashing power of your hardware, the efficiency of the hardware, energy costs, and the price of

Litecoin. It's good to note that while the current price of Litecoin might make mining unprofitable, the price might skyrocket in the future, thus making the whole operation profitable if the miner sells at the right price.

If you are mining solo, you will earn 25 Litecoins every time you discover a block. The value of one Litecoin currently stands at $199, which means that you will get $4975 every time you discover a block. However, it might take you quite a long time before you discover your first block. Also keep in mind that the block reward reduces by half after every 840,000 blocks, with the next halving predicted to take place in 2019. If you are part of mining pool, the payout you receive will depend on the number of people in the pool, as well as the rules of the pool.

Apart from the costs of acquiring your mining hardware, you also need to factor the electricity costs into your profitability. If you want to maximize on profitability, you need to have an efficient rig that does not consume too much power. This depends on its power supply requirements, as well as the number of graphics cards you are using.

Chapter Six: Understanding The Impact Of SegWit And Lightning Network On Litecoin

I have mentioned SegWit several times in this book, and you might be wondering what it is. SegWit (Segregated Witness) is a blockchain upgrade that was meant for Bitcoin. Since Litecoin is an offshoot of Bitcoin, most of the changes on the Bitcoin blockchain could be implemented on the Litecoin blockchain as well. Owing to Litecoin's smaller community and the leadership of Charles Lee, Litecoin was able to implement SegWit before Bitcoin. To help you clearly understand what SegWit is, I will first look at the Bitcoin challenges that necessitated its development.

In the first chapter, I mentioned that Litecoin was developed to solve the challenges faced by Bitcoin. One of these challenges was slow transaction speeds. In recent times, Bitcoin has become even slower, with transactions taking hours to get confirmed instead of the initial 10 minutes. This is because Bitcoin has been nearing its 1MB block size limit. As more and more people join the Bitcoin network, the transactions increase and the amount of data contained in each block becomes heavier, thus clogging and slowing down the network. Therefore, there was need to find a solution to make the network faster if Bitcoin was to see mass adoption. SegWit was developed as the solution that would make Bitcoin faster and more scalable.

Each block is composed of two elements, the header and the body. The header contains the time stamp, the cryptographic hash of the preceding block, and other data. The body contains data about the transaction, including the sender's and recipient's wallet addresses. Instead of having all this data stored in the block, the SegWit modification provides a way to change the amount of data that is stored within each block. SegWit breaks the data stored in the block into two parts which are stored separately. The first part is the transaction data, which contains the sender's and recipient's public keys. The scripts and signatures are then stored separately in an extended 'witness' block – hence the term 'Segregated Witness'. This frees up some space in the original block, allowing it to store data more efficiently.

Litecoin does not have the block size and scaling problems experienced by Bitcoin, so you might be wondering why SegWit was implemented on Litecoin. SegWit provides several advantages besides enabling scaling. One of the major advantages is that it fixes a problem known as transaction malleability.

Litecoin transactions use something known as a transaction identifier to prove the validity of the transaction. The transaction identifier is a 64-digit hexadecimal hash that is derived from the Litecoins being spent, as well as the data of the wallet that will be authorized to spend the outcome of the transaction. Unfortunately, there is a vulnerability that allows small modifications to be made to the transaction, thus changing the transaction identifier while retaining the meaning of the transaction. This is referred to as third party malleability. For instance, a sender might make a transaction and submit it to the network. However, a node, miner, or other third party might modify the transaction slightly. In such a situation, you still send the same Litecoins to the same recipient, but your transaction gets confirmed under a totally different transaction identifier.

Alternatively, if one or more of the transaction signatures is revised, the transaction still remains valid and sends the specified amount of Litecoins to the same recipient, but it is verified under a different transaction identifier. This is because the signatures form part of the identifier. In situations where the transaction identifier changes as a result of a change in signature data, this is known as ScriptSig malleability.

SegWit eliminates the possibility of third party and scriptSig malleability by segregating the malleable parts of the transaction and moving them into a separate witness block. This means that the changes to the witness have no impact on the transaction identifier. Doing so provides benefits to the following parties:

Wallet authors: The simplest way for a user to monitor the status of their outgoing transactions is to look the up using the transaction identifier. However, if a system is vulnerable to third party malleability, this is impossible, therefore forcing the wallet to implement some extra code that keeps track of changed transaction identifiers.

People spending unconfirmed transactions: Let's assume that person A sends Litecoins to person B. Person B then sends the same Litecoins to person C. If the transaction identifier from person A changes due as a result of malleability, then the transaction from person B to person C gets marked as invalid. Person C receives no Litecoins, unless person B decides to send them again.

The Lightning Network: With the problem of malleability eliminated, it becomes easier to make transactions on the Lightning Network. The Lightning Network can run lightweight clients without having to run the full Litecoin blockchain.

Anyone using the blockchain: Without the risk of malleability, it becomes easier to understand, design, and monitor smart contracts.

Apart from eliminating malleability, SegWit also allows faster confirmation of transactions. This in turn reduces transaction fees.

Lightning Network

One of the greatest advantages of SegWit being implemented on the Litecoin blockchain is that it made it possible for the Lightning Network to be implemented as well. The Lightning Network enables faster, cheaper, and more scalable transactions by allowing users to make multiple transactions through a multisig address. Lightning Network also allows atomic cross-chain swaps where Litecoin can be swapped for another cryptocurrency such as Bitcoin without having to go through an exchange or other third party. The first cross-chain atomic swap between Litecoin and Bitcoin was successfully completed in 2017. Finally, the Lightning Network allows the execution of smart contracts on the Litecoin blockchain, which makes it possible for micro-payments to be sent almost instantly. Without this, micro-payments are impractical since the fees might exceed the transaction itself.

To make the Lightning Network easier to understand, I will break it down into two parts. Part 1 will look at multisig addresses, which are the foundation of the Lightning Network. The second part will look at how Lightning Network transactions occur.

Understanding Multisig Addresses

Multisig is short for 'multiple signatures'. Therefore, a multisig address is one that is controlled by multiple people. You can receive Litecoins on a multisig wallet the same way you can on a regular wallet. However, certain conditions have to be met before you can spend the Litecoins from a multisig wallet. To make it easier to understand, I will use an illustration. Let's assume that three people decide to come together to set up a multisig address. They can set it up in such a way that either one, two, or all three of them have to sign the transaction before Litecoins can be sent from the address. By setting up these conditions, these people are essentially creating a smart contract.

Let's assume that the three people set up their multisig wallet so that each transaction has to be signed by the three of them. If one person makes a payment from the address, an open payment channel is created. This means that a transaction has been started but is yet to be completed. When an open payment channel is created, the Litecoins are locked within the wallet. A proposal is also sent to the other two people to sign off the pending payment. The payment will not be added to the blockchain because it is yet to be completed. The payment channel will be closed once all the three owners sign off the transaction. Once the payment channel is closed, the Litecoins are released and sent to the recipient. The transaction is also added to the blockchain and the necessary fees taken and paid to miners who verify the transaction.

Lightning Network Transactions

I mentioned earlier that one of the advantages of Lightning Network is that is it cheaper when making multiple, small-size transactions. Let us take a look at how this works. Let's assume person A and person B are conducting business that requires person A to pay person B 1 Litecoin for 10 projects. Instead of paying 0.1 Litecoin with the requisite transaction fees for every completed project, the two of them can opt to use the Lightning Network, allowing person A to pay person B 10 times while paying a single transaction fee. In order to do this, the two of them will set up a multisig address that requires both their signatures for Litecoins to be sent. Person A then sends 1 Litecoin into the multisig address and creates a smart contract states that the 1 Litecoin will be sent back to her personal address if it is still in the address after a certain period of time.

When person B delivers the first project, person A makes a payment of 0.1 Litecoins to person B, thereby opening a payment channel. At this point, person B has two options. They can either sign the transaction and accept the payment or ignore it and leave it open. If person B signs the payment, they will receive the 0.1 Litecoins, the payment channel will close, the multisig will have 0.9 Litecoins remaining and a transaction fee will be paid to miners. However, if person B ignores the transaction, the payment channel remains open and other transactions can still be made. Once person B delivers project number two, person A will make another payment of 0.2 Litecoins to person B. At this point, there are two existing payments, one for 0.1 Litecoins and another for 0.2 Litecoins. However, once one of these transactions is signed and closed, the other disappears. Therefore, if person B were to accept the payment, he would sign the second transaction and receive 0.2 Litecoins for the two delivered projects. After signing the second transaction, the first transaction of 0.1 Litecoin will disappear.

However, person B can still choose to ignore the payment and deliver the third project. Person A would then make another payment of 0.3 Litecoins. All the three payments would be open for person B to sign. Let's assume this goes on until person B delivers all 10 projects. Person A would then make a payment of 1 Litecoin, creating 10 open transactions. It's important to note that at this point, no transaction has been added to the Litecoin blockchain and no fee has been charged, since the payment channels are still open. These are what are referred to as 'offchain' transactions, since they are made without being recorded on the blockchain.

Once person A has made the final 1 Litecoin transaction for the 10 projects, person B signs the last transaction. When he does this, the other 9 open transactions disappear. Person B receives 1 Litecoin and the payment channel is closed. The transaction is finally added to the Litecoin blockchain and only one transaction fee is paid to the miners. In addition, only one transaction is recorded on the blockchain instead of 10 individual transactions. This in turn significantly reduces the size of the block since fewer transactions are recorded. With the Lighting Network, it's also possible for person B to initiate a payment, since he also has control over the multisig address. However, the transaction will only be completed after person A signs it as well.

The Lightning Network makes it possible for Litecoin to be used for device-to-device transactions, at retail point of sale terminals and any other place where instant payments may be required. This will make Litecoin very competitive in the long term as a payment platform and gives it the potential to bring a revolution to peer-to-peer payment systems. The Lightning Network also allows machine-to-machine Litecoin payments. To do these, the smart contract framework would be implemented, enabling firms running automated processes to create direct payment connections between their software and the software being run by their clients or suppliers.

Chapter Seven: The Future Of Litecoin

At the moment, Litecoin is the sixth largest cryptocurrency, with a market cap of about $10 billion. It saw massive growth in 2017, with its value growing over 9000% from about $4 per Litecoin to an all-time high of $371. Its growth in the past year outperformed the growth of other popular cryptocurrencies, including Bitcoin and Ethereum. Despite all this growth, the best is yet to come. There are still several reasons why the future of Litecoin looks bright. Below are some of the factors that will push the growth of Litecoin in 2018 and beyond, as well as some predictions as to the future of Litecoin.

MAST

Despite being quite impressive and useful, the blockchain technology on which Litecoin is built is still in its early stages, both in terms of development and adoption. Many more technologies are being developed with the aim of making the blockchain faster, more secure, and more efficient. One of these technologies is known as MAST. The Term MAST stands for Merkelized Abstract Syntax Trees. The implementation of MAST on Litecoin will improve its speed, privacy, and scalability. What MAST does is combine multiple hashed data strings (Merkle Trees) into a single, smaller output known as a Merkle root.

MAST also makes it possible for smart contracts to be efficiently employed on the Litecoin blockchain. Currently, smart contracts can be employed on the Litecoin blockchain. However, they take a lot of space, since every smart contract is readily visible on the blockchain. With MAST, space can be saved on the chain, since only complete smart contracts are revealed. Nodes can verify transactions by reading only the top layer of the Merkle Tree, without knowing the contents of the entire Merkle Tree.

MAST also improves privacy since it combines individual transactions data sets into a single compact hash known as the Merkle Root. However, it would be impossible to recreate the Merkle Root to come up with the original data. As more and more people adopt cryptocurrencies, governments will definitely want to get involved in order to tax the billions being made from the industry. By implementing MAST, which improves privacy, Litecoin will attract more users who want to fly under the government's radar.

To illustrate the above, let's assume a smart contract where person A sends 10 Litecoins to person B only if person B fulfills a certain condition. If person B does not fulfill the condition, the 10 Litecoins are refunded to person A. With MAST, this data is combined with data sets from several other smart contracts and hashed through a Merkle Tree. The result is a Merkle root that is significantly smaller than the Merkle tree. This smaller Merkle root is then recorded on the blockchain. The transactions can be verified through the Merkle root but it would be impossible for any other entity who did not know any of the input data to decipher the contents of the Merkle root. This way, the Merkle root saves space on the chain while providing a higher level of anonymity for persons A and B.

It's important to note that MAST is not what makes it possible to implement smart contracts on the Litecoin blockchain. Instead, MAST takes advantage of Merkle trees to enable large, complex smart contracts to be recorded on the blockchain as a single, much smaller Merkle root. The implementation of MAST is likely to lead to increased adoption of Litecoin.

Lightning Network

We have already discussed what the Lightning Network is and how it benefits the Litecoin blockchain. While the Lightning Network has already been implemented on the Litecoin blockchain, it is still in testing mode. Once the Lightning Network is fully implemented on the network, it will make Litecoin a lot faster, cheaper, and more scalable. We can expect the adoption and value of Litecoin to increase following the full-scale implementation of the Lightning Network. A prototype wallet for the Lightning

Network is also being developed. This will also push the adoption of Litecoin.

Atomic Swaps

This is another technology that has already been trialed on the Litecoin network. By successfully testing atomic swaps, Litecoin has already set the pace for other cryptocurrencies. The cryptocurrency community has been looking forward to the day when P2P transactions will make cryptocurrency exchanges unnecessary. Litecoin has brought this day closer. However, the test atomic swap was not done on the Lightning Network, but rather on-chain. Litecoin is hoping to stabilize the implementation of the Lightning Network, which will in turn allow atomic swaps to be done on the Lightning Network. The end result will be instantaneous P2P trades that take place at almost zero cost. There is still plenty of work to be done, but once this comes to fruition, it will be a very major win for Litecoin and any other cryptocurrency that will implement it successfully.

Covenants

While it does not seem to be a top priority upgrade at the moment, the implementation of covenants will also have very big impact on the Litecoin ecosystem. In historical English Common Law, a covenant is a solemn promise to do something or to refrain from doing something. In Property Law, a covenant is a set of conditions that affect how a parcel of land will be used. Litecoin covenants are a set a conditions that make it possible to restrict the future use of Litecoins once a transaction is completed. Covenants make it possible to lump together Litecoins and bind them into blocks. This way, a user can bind together their Litecoins, making it impossible for them to get mixed up with other Litecoins from other transactions in the network. Covenants will make it possible for other upgrades like the 'Colored Coin Protocol' and 'Vaults' to be implemented on the Litecoin network.

Vaults will increase the security of the Litecoin network by making it possible for a user to lock up their Litecoins even in the event that a malicious person steals the coins. They will do this by building in some sort of delay for transactions that are carried out by an assailant. However, the rightful owner of the Litecoins will have a master key which they can use to speed up the transaction. The Covenant upgrade is a pretty complicated solution, which explains why the Litecoin team does not consider it to be a high priority upgrade.

Colored Coin Protocol

I mentioned above that the implementation of Litecoin Covenants will make it possible to implement the Colored Coin Protocol. This is an upgrade that will make it possible to attach a 'distinguishable mark' to specific Litecoins. This gives users more control over their Litecoins. Normally, when you send Litecoins, they get mixed up with Litecoins from other transactions on the network. By 'coloring' them with a distinguishable mark, your Litecoins can be tracked and retrieved.

The Colored Coins Protocol has a number of applications. An obvious one is that they can be attached to an asset, allowing Litecoin to be used the same way Ether is used to create ICO utility tokens. Colored coins could also be linked to a physical asset. For instance, a specific Litecoin can be assigned to a computerized car model like the Tesla. This specific Litecoin would then act as a key to the car. Alternatively, some Litecoins could be attached to a certain amount of gold that is held by a trusted party. The Litecoins would represent ownership of the gold. Trading the Litecoins would be easier than trading in the actual gold. The Litecoin blockchain would act as the settlement and dispute resolution mechanism. This would allow physical assets to be transferred at low fees and with minimal validation times. Combine this with the Lightning Network and it presents a very powerful use case for Litecoin.

Another use case for Colored Coins would be to combine them with smart contracts, giving them some sort of self-termination. For instance, let's assume some travelers want to rent an Airbnb for a week. The host would send them colored coins that are set to self-terminate after seven days. The Litecoins would act as keys, giving the travelers access to the house. After seven days, the colored coins would self-terminate, thereby denying access to the travelers in case they attempt to illegally extend their stay.

Like the Covenant upgrade, the Colored Coins Protocol is not a top priority project for the Litecoin development team. This is because it depends on covenants, and therefore can only be implemented after the implementation of covenants.

Confidential Transactions

While cryptocurrencies charmed the world with the promise of anonymity, many major cryptocurrencies, including Litecoin and Bitcoin, do not have any serious privacy features. They do not make an attempt to completely mask users' identities. However, Litecoin is on the way to improving the privacy of its users by implementing Confidential Transactions (CT). Litecoin, which has become the testing ground for cutting-edge features, is borrowing this technology from another altcoin called Monero. Monero is a privacy-oriented cryptocurrency that has been using Ring Signatures to enable Confidential Transactions.

Charles Lee is a huge fan of Confidential Transactions and has already stated that the Litecoin development team is working on making this upgrade. By implementing Confidential Transactions, the amounts involved in Litecoin transactions will only be visible to those involved in the transaction and any parties that they might share the information with. According to Lee, Confidential Transactions will be integrated into the Litecoin network through a soft fork. However, there are no specific timelines for the implementation of this new feature.

The implementation of Confidential Transactions on Litecoin is going to produce mixed reactions. On one hand, tracing transactions will be more difficult, which will increase users' level of privacy. On the other hand, the increased privacy might attract criminals to Litecoin. According to Lee, the aim of implementing Confidential Transactions is not to make Litecoin the go-to cryptocurrency for criminals. The feature will only be optional on the network, with those who want the benefits of the feature having to pay a higher fee. The aim of introducing this feature is to make Litecoins fungible.

Introducing Confidential Transactions on Litecoin will also have another major benefit. Currently, fiat currencies are backed by the central banks of the printing nation. In times of financial crisis, like the Asian Financial crisis of 1997, there is mass devaluation of fiat currencies in these nations. The savings of regular people in these nations get entirely wiped out, and many companies go bankrupt. However, if currencies were not backed by nations, they would freely flow across borders, which would insulate them against such devaluation in times of financial crisis. With Confidential Transactions, it will be difficult for governments to trace the flow of money in the form of Litecoins across borders. This means that people will be able to use Litecoins as a hedge against the inflation of their national fiat currencies.

The Rate Of Litecoin Adoption Will Increase

Owing to the abundant supply of Litecoins and the significantly fast transaction speeds, you can expect that the number of people using Litecoin will keep increasing. In addition, it's also good to keep in mind that the use of Litecoins as well as other altcoins is tied to the use of Bitcoin. The more people that use Bitcoin, the more they adopt Litecoins and the other altcoins. You can easily note this by comparing the price charts of Bitcoin and Litecoin. The correlation is unmistakable.

However, with Litecoin having successfully trialed and started the implementation of SegWit and the Lightning Network, in addition to the host of other exciting features that are in the pipeline, Litecoin has a higher scaling potential as compared to Bitcoin.

From the information in this chapter, it is clear that the coming year holds a lot in store for Litecoin. It's safe to assume that we will see many more developments and upgrades on the Litecoin network. Litecoin is still in its early stages and institutional money is yet to get into it. Once the network develops infrastructure that makes it easier for institutional and retail investors to get into Litecoin, there is no doubt that it is going to explode. With all these updates being rolled out and the able leadership of Charles Lee, Litecoin is definitely going to give other cryptocurrencies a run for their (digital) money. In addition, the Litecoin Foundation is helping to raise money that will be used to hire full-time developers to improve on Litecoin's code. The Foundation raises through donations and the sale of Litecoin-branded funds. Lee has also stated that the Litecoin development team is looking at potential scaling solutions, though Litecoin does not need any scaling solutions at the moment. If Litecoin continues along its current growth trajectory, it might soon need a scaling solution, therefore it's good that the team is planning ahead.

Despite The Optimism, Certainty Is Impossible

While enthusiasts and industry experts are generally optimistic about the future of Litecoin, it's good to keep in mind that it is impossible to make predictions about the future of Litecoin – or any other cryptocurrency, for that matter – with absolute certainty. Apart from the technological and feature upgrades, the future of Litecoin also depends on government regulations, especially in countries that are key players in the cryptocurrency space, such as Japan, China, and the US. A good example is how China banned cryptocurrencies in 2017, leading to the plummeting of the prices of most cryptocurrencies.

It might sound surprising that government regulations can affect the future of Litecoin and other cryptocurrencies when they are supposed to be decentralized. However, it is important to note that cryptocurrencies are not above government regulations. For instance, it a government prohibits companies within its jurisdiction from accepting Litecoin payments, this would affect the adoption of Litecoin. Similarly, the closing of cryptocurrency exchanges will impact the adoption and use of Litecoin and other cryptocurrencies.

The massive growths that most cryptocurrencies have experienced has led to the rise of imitators and scammers. The total market capitalization of cryptocurrencies has also grown significantly to the current $600 billion. All these factors have had the effect of putting the cryptocurrency markets in the radar of the SEC and the IRS. For instance, the IRS recently asked Coinbase to submit the names of any investor that made cryptocurrency trades exceeding $20,000 within the last year. As the market capitalization of cryptocurrencies increases, government interest is also going to increase. This makes it impossible to confidently predict the future of Litecoin and other cryptocurrencies.

Chapter Eight: Should You Invest In Litecoin?

For years after its release, Litecoin was largely ignored, staying well in the shadows of Bitcoin. Accordingly, the dollar value of Litecoin remained in the single-digits. However, the last year has seen the value of Litecoin skyrocket. This increase in value has generated a lot of interest. Many investors are now wondering whether they should invest in Bitcoin's younger sibling, hoping that it will maintain its upward trajectory. Before you start investing in Litecoin, however, you should remember that it is a currency. Therefore, investing in Litecoin does not work the same way as investing in stocks or bonds. Instead, you should think of it as investing in the forex market. So, should you invest in Litecoin? Before we can come to a conclusive answer, let's take a look at the factors that are behind Litecoin's bullish run in the last year.

Piggybacking On Bitcoin

The last couple of years have seen increasing support for Bitcoin, both by institutional and retail investors. This in turn drove speculation around the coin and led to an increase in its value. Already, a number of public and private investment institutions including NASDAQ, CBOE, and CME have shown an interest in bringing Bitcoin to the mainstream market. The first Bitcoin futures contracts have also been announced. Aside from showing confidence in Bitcoin, these moves have shown confidence in the entire cryptocurrency space, thus leading to the growth of other cryptocurrencies, including Litecoin.

While there have not been any official plans to bring Litecoin into the options and futures markets any time soon, the incoming wave of institutional money into Bitcoin will continue lifting the other cryptocurrencies as well. With Litecoin being one of the most popular altcoins and a close relative to Bitcoin, it has experienced one of the highest growth rates as a result of growing interest in Bitcoin. You can easily see the evidence of this by comparing Litecoin's and Bitcoin's growth charts.

Increasing Media Coverage

The massive growth of Bitcoin brought a lot of media attention from news outlets, social networks, financial pundits, and more. However, the attention was not solely focused on Bitcoin. Instead, the media attention was focused on the whole cryptocurrency industry. Being one of the very first serious cryptocurrencies to be launched, Litecoin received a huge share of the media attention, which led to growth for the digital currency. This in turn led to more media attention, creating a cycle of increasing prices and increasing media attention.

In addition, Charles Lee has helped the Litecoin network by putting it in the spotlight through shows such as Squawk Box by CNBC, where he explained the differences between Litecoin and Bitcoin. Today, most financial news channels include the price of Litecoin next to Bitcoin, stocks, and other noteworthy assets.

Outlet For Bitcoin's Frustrations

The massive growth of Bitcoin, both in value and adoption, unfortunately exposed some of its major weaknesses. One of these is the scaling challenge, owing to Bitcoin's large block size and confirmation times. The influx of new users to the Bitcoin network has led to unusually high transaction fees and transaction confirmation times of several hours, sometimes even running into days. These frustrations with Bitcoin have led some investors to other cryptocurrencies. Having been developed to provide a solution to Bitcoin's challenges, Litecoin has benefited a lot from these frustrations.

Unlike the very long transaction confirmation times with Bitcoin, Litecoin has a confirmation time of only 2-3 minutes. This is due to Litecoins smaller block size. Litecoin also does not have the exceptionally high transaction times that have become synonymous with Bitcoin. Apart from being an outlet for the frustrations investors experience with Bitcoin, some other investors have also come into Litecoin in order to diversify their cryptocurrency portfolios.

SegWit And Lightning Network

The successful testing of the Lightning Network was a big win for Litecoin. As the news of the Lightning Network and what it means for Litecoin gets published, investors realize that Litecoin has a great future. In addition to being ahead of Bitcoin in terms of transaction confirmation times, Litecoin's early implementation of SegWit and the Lightning Network shows that the network is ready for off-layer storage and processing solution as well. According to industry experts, the benefits brought about by the Lightning Network are what cryptocurrencies need if they are to go mainstream. Having been the first to test the Lightning Network, many investors are confident in the digital currency and have put their money in it, fueling its growth.

Asian Investors

Another major factor that drove Litecoin's massive growth was the increased interest from Asian investors. The value of Litecoin skyrocketed in June 2017 after an influx of South Korean and Chinese investors into the market.

Bithumb, a cryptocurrency exchange based in South Korea, is the second largest Litecoin exchange by trading volume. The largest Litecoin exchange by trading volume is Coinbase's GDAX.

Despite western economies being wary of cryptocurrencies, with some even passing legislations in an attempt to clamp down on them, Asian investors have not shied away from putting their money into this new industry, helping fuel its growth. Most of these investments have been directed towards Bitcoin, Ethereum, and Litecoin.

Fear Of Missing Out

The fear of missing out (FOMO) is a very powerful human emotion and one of the greatest motivations for taking action. While losing money in an investment hurts, to most cryptocurrency traders, nothing is more painful than seeing the price of a coin skyrocket after failing to buy it when the price was cheap, or after selling it at a throwaway price.

The stellar rise of Bitcoin caught many traders by surprise, while some missed out because they couldn't get verified by their exchange of choice in time. However,

Litecoin provided the perfect chance to make a killing on another cryptocurrency. Many amateur traders were attracted by Litecoin's relatively low prices and decided to pump it in order to get the chance they missed with Bitcoin.

How Participants View It

While many traders do not fully grasp the technical differences between Litecoin and its bigger brother, they have not shied away from investing their money in Litecoin, regardless. Most of these investments are driven by the behavior of its price relative to other cryptocurrencies. Being a coin that has been in the market for quite a while, Litecoin is seen as being as accessible as Bitcoin.

Apart from the distinct technical advantages Litecoin offers over Bitcoin, the Litecoin community has also benefitted from the growing adoption of the coin by the ecommerce sector. Litecoin is quickly cementing a place for itself as one of the top cryptocurrencies, even as a funding tool. Many ecommerce sites that accept Bitcoin also accept

Litecoin, while some new cryptocurrencies have started accepting Litecoin during their token sales, in addition to Bitcoin and Ethereum. This is because of Litecoin's broadening appeal and its significantly low transfer costs.

The adoption of Litecoin has also been driven by its relatively drama-free community, which has given the coin a steady trend and less volatility. This has made Litecoin a great option for spending, trading, arbitration, and even fundraising. Experienced cryptocurrency traders have compared Litecoin's market cap to Bitcoin's, and based on Litecoins advantages and its higher maximum number of coins, they see Litecoin as a very undervalued cryptocurrency. However, with all the progress and upgrades that are in store, Litecoin has the potential to evolve into one of the largest cryptocurrencies.

So, Should You Invest In Litecoin?

If you are interested in investing your money in Litecoin, you should approach your investment in the same manner you would approach any other investment that is highly speculative in nature. This means that you should realize that there is a very high risk that you might end up losing a huge chunk of your money, if not all of it. Remember, the intrinsic value of a cryptocurrency is what a person is willing to pay for it at that particular moment. This explains why cryptocurrencies are very susceptible to volatility, which translates to a higher chance of profit as well as a huge risk of loss for you as an investor. For instance, on 16 January 2018, the price of Litecoin plunged from $225 to $152 within a couple of hours. If you are not ready for this kind of volatility, you should probably seek other investment options that are better suited to you.

However, if you still want to invest in cryptocurrencies, here are some reasons why you should put your money into Litecoin:

- Litecoin is one of the first altcoins to be developed, so it has been around for quite some time. This means that the coin is not a scam. It is also evidence of a good community behind the coin.
- The Litecoin blockchain is one of the most secure, second only to Bitcoin.
- The Litecoin blockchain is similar to Bitcoin's. This means that the trust people put in Bitcoin and its

adoption rate will most likely reflect on Litecoin as well.

- Litecoin was developed to have much faster transaction confirmation times, right from its inception.

- Owing to its smaller community and a visible and vocal leader, Litecoin is usually the first cryptocurrency to implement blockchain improvements. For instance, Litecoin was the first cryptocurrency to activate SegWit, making its transactions even faster. In addition, it was the first one to test Lightning Network, which is due to be fully implemented soon. Litecoin has established itself as the testing ground for improvements before they are rolled out on Bitcoin.

- Like Bitcoin, Litecoin has a maximum number of coins to be released within its lifetime. This will help hedge the coin against inflation.

- Litecoin can now be bought and sold on Coinbase. Coinbase is one of the best cryptocurrency exchanges in the world. It does not support any altcoins that pop up out of the blue. By adopting

Litecoin, it shows that Coinbase believes in the coin.

- By adopting Litecoin, Coinbase made Litecoin more accessible to Americans as well as several other countries that are supported by the exchange. This will likely lead to more adoption for the digital currency, as well as an increase in price.

- In the past three or so years, Litecoin has enjoyed relative stability. Amid the crazy volatility experienced by other cryptocurrencies, including Bitcoin and Ethereum, its stability makes it a viable digital asset to invest in.

- The value of Litecoin is low compared to that of Bitcoin. Therefore, Litecoin provides a very viable alternative for people who want to get into cryptocurrency trading but who do not have enough money to invest in Bitcoin.

- The Litecoin community is rapidly growing. If the experiences of Bitcoin are anything to go by, massive growth in Litecoin's community will lead to similar growth in its value. Already, the Litecoin community is quite big, and there are lots of investments in the coin, so the possibility that it might fail is very low. People can no longer brush Litecoin aside as a pump and dump or a scam. People are starting to see that the cryptocurrency has real value.

Bubble Concerns

For several months now, there have been claims by market observers that cryptocurrencies have entered a bubble. Many cryptocurrencies have been in a very strong bullish run throughout the whole of 2017, something that has been used as evidence to back the claim that the prices of cryptocurrencies have become inflated. According to a recent survey by Natixis, 64% of institutional investors believe that cryptocurrencies are in a bubble. According to some cryptocurrency enthusiasts and traders, not only is the market in a bubble, but there is also a high likelihood that the bubble will burst in the near future. Already, the prices of popular cryptocurrencies, including Bitcoin, Litecoin, and Ethereum, have started falling after hitting all-time highs in December 2017. People are comparing the rise in cryptocurrency markets to the dotcom bubble, which was characterized by an unprecedented rise followed by a huge plummeting of stock prices. Many people lost everything, but in the end, technologies and companies that transformed the society emerged. The most important thing is that, before investing in any cryptocurrency, you should do your research and understand the underlying technology. Most of all, avoid investing based on hype.

Conclusion

As one the first cryptocurrencies to be launched, Litecoin is rapidly attracting the attention of the media, as well as retail and institutional investors. Owing to the technical advantages it has over Bitcoin, people have realized that Litecoin has a place in the future of cryptocurrency. In addition, Litecoin has a very strong leadership in the form of its founder, former Google programmer Charles Lee. Having already started the implementation of awesome upgrades like SegWit, having successfully tested new technologies like Lightning Network, and with a slew of other upgrades in the pipeline, there is no doubt that the future is bright for Litecoin. Litecoin is also significantly cheaper than Bitcoin, which makes it more affordable for investors who do not have huge sums of money to invest in cryptocurrency. I hope that after reading this book, you have learned everything you need to know about Litecoin. However, always remember that investing in any cryptocurrency, including Litecoin, is a risky affair. Only invest money that you can afford to lose.

If you enjoyed this book, please take the time to leave me a review on Amazon. I appreciate your honest feedback, and it helps me to continue producing high-quality books.

Other Ikuya Takashima books availabe on Amazon.

Cryptocurrency: How I Paid my 6 Figure Divorce Settlement by Cryptocurrency Investing, Cryptocurrency Trading

Ethereum: The Ultimate Guide to the World of Ethereum, Ethereum Mining, Ethereum Investing, Smart Contracts, Dapps and DAOs, Ether, Blockchain Technology

Blockchain: The Ultimate Guide To The World Of Blockchain Technology, Bitcoin, Ethereum, Cryptocurrency, Smart Contracts

Bitcoin: The Ultimate Guide to the World of Bitcoin, Bitcoin Mining, Bitcoin Investing, Blockchain Technology, Cryptocurrency

ICO: The Ultimate Guide To Investing In ICOs, ICO Investing, Initial Coin Offering, Cryptocurrency Investing, Investing In Cryptocurrrency

Ripple: The Ultimate Guide to the World of Ripple XRP, Ripple Investing, Ripple Coin, Ripple Cryptocurrency, Cryptocurrency

About The Author

31-year-old Ikuya Takashima is a Software Developer, entrepreneur, investor and author.

Ikuya first entered the world of Cryptocurrency in 2014 when he finally decided to invest in Bitcoin after several years of following the online currency. Ikuya is now a Cryptocurrency expert & enthusiast with an impressive Cryptocurrency portfolio and investments in several Bitcoin & Ethereum startups.

Ikuya's latest venture is to share his knowledge and passion on the world of Cryptocurrencies with the goal of making seemingly complex and intimidating topics simple and easy-to-read.

In Ikuya's spare time he likes to read, travel and spend time with family and friends.

www.ingramcontent.com/pod-product-compliance
Lightning Source LLC
Chambersburg PA
CBHW070147230526
45471CB00002B/551